USBORNE

HOW YOUR BODY WORKS

Judy Hindley
Assisted by Christopher Rawson

Illustrated by Colin King
Designed by John Jamieson, Geoff Davies
and Fiona Brown

Medical adviser: Susan Jenkins, MRCP, DCH
Educational adviser: Paula Varrow

CONTENTS

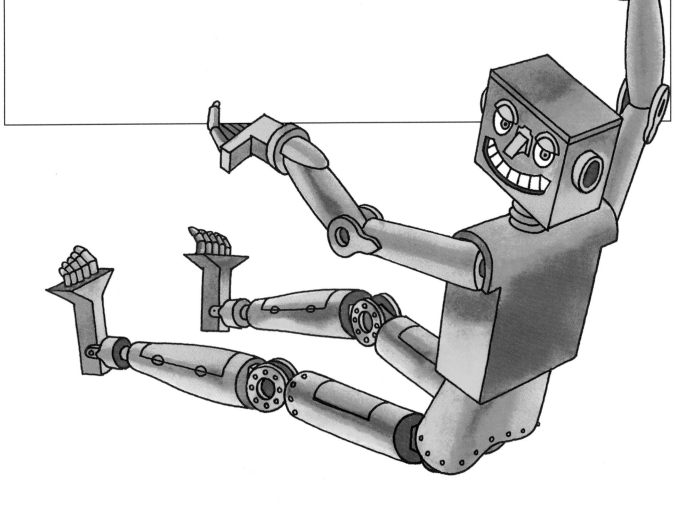

ABOUT THIS BOOK

In many ways, your body is like a wonderful machine. It can do hundreds of different kinds of jobs. To show how it does some of its most important jobs, we have invented lots of different machines.

Our machines do not connect with each other. Each is separate, and each can do only some of the jobs your body can do.

Real machines are much better than bodies at doing some things. Computers can calculate faster. Cranes can lift heavier loads. Cars can move faster.

But your body fits together so well that it can do many different jobs – and it can do lots of them at the same time.

No scientist has ever been able to make a machine as neat and light as your body that could do even half the things your body does. And no machine can have new ideas, or make jokes, or change its mind – or have babies.

Eating Machine

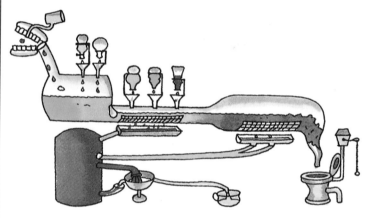

Our Eating Machine (pages 4 and 5) shows what your body does to food after you swallow it.

Teeth and Tongue Machine

Our Teeth and Tongue Machine (pages 6 and 7) is a completely separate machine. We made it to show what different teeth do.

Breathing Machine

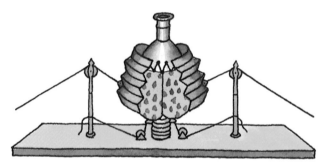

Our Breathing Machine (pages 12 and 13) shows how your ribs work with a special muscle to make you breathe.

Mechanical Man

We made up a Mechanical Man (pages 28 to 31) so that we could show how other muscles work to move your bones.

AN EATING MACHINE

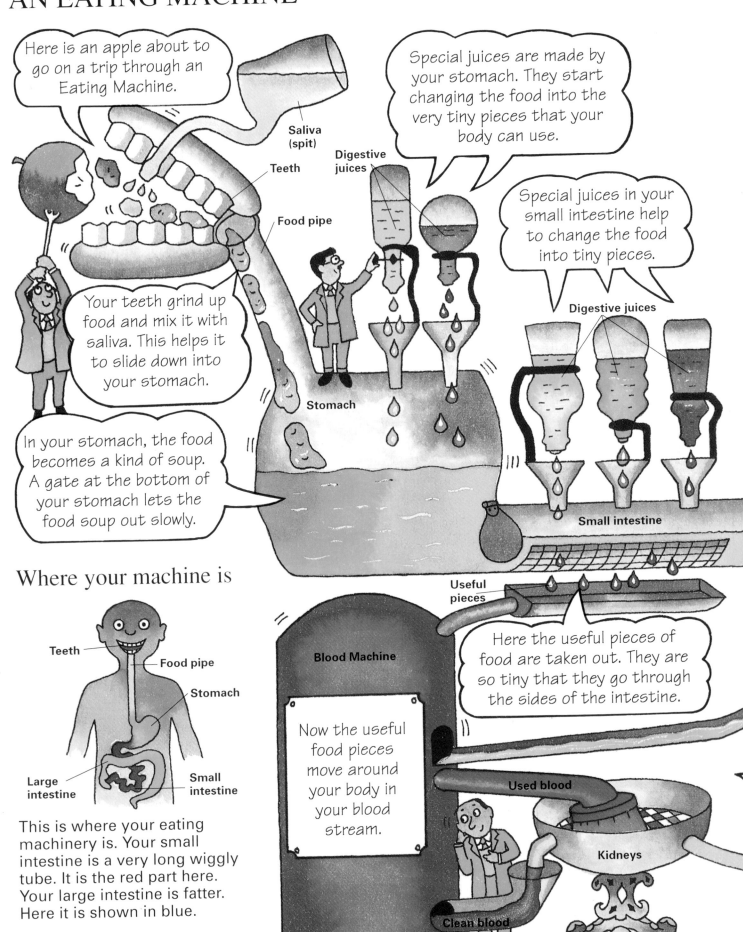

Here is an apple about to go on a trip through an Eating Machine.

Saliva (spit)

Teeth

Food pipe

Your teeth grind up food and mix it with saliva. This helps it to slide down into your stomach.

In your stomach, the food becomes a kind of soup. A gate at the bottom of your stomach lets the food soup out slowly.

Special juices are made by your stomach. They start changing the food into the very tiny pieces that your body can use.

Digestive juices

Special juices in your small intestine help to change the food into tiny pieces.

Digestive juices

Stomach

Small intestine

Useful pieces

Here the useful pieces of food are taken out. They are so tiny that they go through the sides of the intestine.

Blood Machine

Now the useful food pieces move around your body in your blood stream.

Used blood

Kidneys

Clean blood

Where your machine is

Teeth

Food pipe

Stomach

Large intestine

Small intestine

This is where your eating machinery is. Your small intestine is a very long wiggly tube. It is the red part here. Your large intestine is fatter. Here it is shown in blue.

4

Here is a machine we have invented to show the main things that happen to the food you eat.

In food there are things your body can use and things it cannot use. In your own eating machinery, the food is chopped and churned and changed into tiny pieces by special juices. This is called digestion.

Then the useful things can be sorted out and sent where they are needed.

To get rid of bad food, muscles in your chest and near your stomach squeeze together. The gate at the end of your stomach stays shut, so the food goes up.

Chest squeezes down.

Muscle squeezes up.

Stomach juices mixed with the food make it taste sour.

Gate stays shut.

Large intestine

The waste is very sludgy by the time it gets here. You get rid of it when you go to the toilet.

Water

Water is taken out through the sides here. It becomes part of your blood.

Used blood is cleaned by the kidneys. Clean blood goes back into the blood stream. Waste water goes into the toilet.

A TEETH AND TONGUE MACHINE

This Teeth and Tongue Machine gets food ready to be swallowed. It does the main things your real teeth and tongue do.

This machine has a chopper and some grinding wheels. You have special kinds of teeth to do what these parts do. In the box on the opposite page, you can see what they look like, how many of each kind you have, and where they are in your mouth.

Your front teeth have sharp edges to chop off bites.

Chopper

Tongue

Your tongue carries food to your grinders. It takes the mashed-up bites to the back of your throat when you swallow.

Why do teeth turn bad?

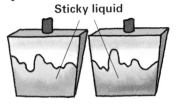

Sticky liquid

Liquid from chewed food sticks to teeth. You cannot see it but your teeth may feel sticky if you slide your tongue around.

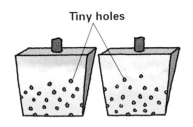

Tiny holes

If the stickiness stays, it makes tiny holes in your teeth. This is a little like rust on metal tools when they are left wet.

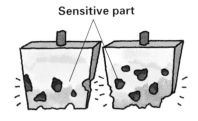

Sensitive part

Germs in the air make the holes deeper. When they reach the sensitive part under the hard part of your teeth, they hurt.

How are teeth mended?

Drill out the bad part!

Germs live in holes in bad teeth. They eat the good part, which makes deeper holes. Dentists drill out the bad parts.

Fill in the holes!

The hard outside of teeth cannot grow back. Dentists have to fill the holes with metal to keep the germs out.

What are fangs for?

Fangs are the pointy teeth next to the choppers. Some animals use fangs to stab and grip prey. We do not use our fangs much.

Saliva helps the food to slide around your mouth and between your teeth.

A kind of trap door at the back of your throat closes your windpipe when you swallow.

Grinders

Tongue

Trap door

Windpipe   Food pipe

Your back teeth are bumpy on top. You can feel this. They work together, grinding food between the bumps.

Your bumpy grinders need careful cleaning when they finish work. Food often sticks between the bumps.

Count the teeth

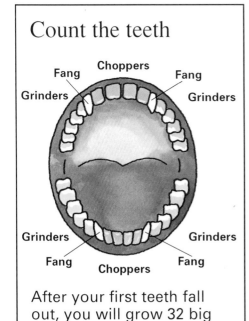

Choppers
Fang   Fang
Grinders   Grinders

Grinders   Grinders
Fang   Fang
Choppers

After your first teeth fall out, you will grow 32 big teeth. Your jaw has to grow too, so they can fit in. This picture shows how many of each kind will grow.

Tongues and tasting

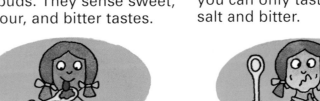

Salty ham

Sweet ice cream

Sour lemon

Bitter orange peel

Nerves from your tongue carry messages to your brain. The nerves come from spots called taste buds. They sense sweet, salt, sour, and bitter tastes.

Your nose tells your brain about many food tastes. If you hold your nose while you eat, you can only taste sweet, sour, salt and bitter.

There are patches of different kinds of taste buds on your tongue. There are lots of sweet-tasters on the tip.

Bitter-tasters are near the back of your tongue. Often you do not notice a bitter taste until you are ready to swallow.

7

WHAT IS BLOOD?

Most of your blood is a clear liquid called plasma. The red cells in blood make it look red. Blood is crowded with special cells doing different kinds of work. This picture shows some of the things they do.

Your body needs food and a special gas called oxygen to live and grow and work. Your blood stream flows around your body like a river, to bring supplies to all the body cells. There is more about your blood stream on pages 10-11.

How blood gets oxygen...

Red blood cells bring waste gas to your lungs. They exchange it for oxygen.

The air you breathe into your lungs carries oxygen. The air you breathe out takes away waste gas.

...and water...

Lots of water goes into your blood through the eating machinery. More than half of your blood is made of water.

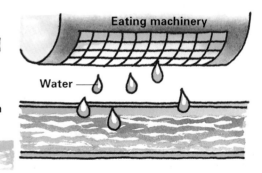

Your body is made of tiny parts called cells. Page 45 shows you more about cells.

Group of body cells

IN OUT

IN OUT

What blood looks like

Cells are so small you need a very strong microscope to see them. Under a microscope a drop of blood looks like this.

Plasma

White blood cell

Red blood cells

The blood takes away any waste made by the cells. It is cleaned as it goes through your kidneys. Page 4 shows you more about this.

Waste

Food

Plasma

Pieces of food are carried by your blood stream. The body cells pick up what they need as the blood flows past.

Waste gas

OUT

These red blood cells are carrying waste gas. They will exchange it for oxygen in your lungs and then come back.

How blood gets food

Your blood carries pieces of food to your liver, which sorts the food. It changes some of it to prepare it for your body.

Your liver stores some pieces of food and sends other pieces back into your blood.

Your blood carries food from your liver to where your body needs it.

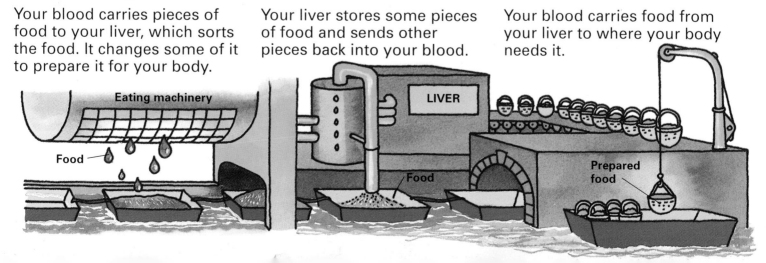

Eating machinery

Food

LIVER

Food

Prepared food

HOW BLOOD GOES AROUND

Your blood stream has many tiny branches. The branches join in a complicated network so that the blood goes around and around your body. The map of a big toe at the bottom of the page shows how the branches join.

Your heart is a pump that keeps blood flowing around. It squeezes out blood like a squeezy bottle. It sends blood to your lungs to get rid of waste gas and pick up oxygen. It sends blood around your body to take oxygen to all the cells in your body.

Your blood goes through rubbery pipes called blood vessels. Page 44 shows where your main blood vessels are.

How your heart works

The top squeezes.

Your heart is a muscle with four tubes, as shown above. The tubes are big blood vessels. The picture below shows where they lead.

Then the bottom squeezes.

When your heart squeezes, it pumps blood out and sucks it in through different tubes. Tiny gates open and shut in your heart while this happens.

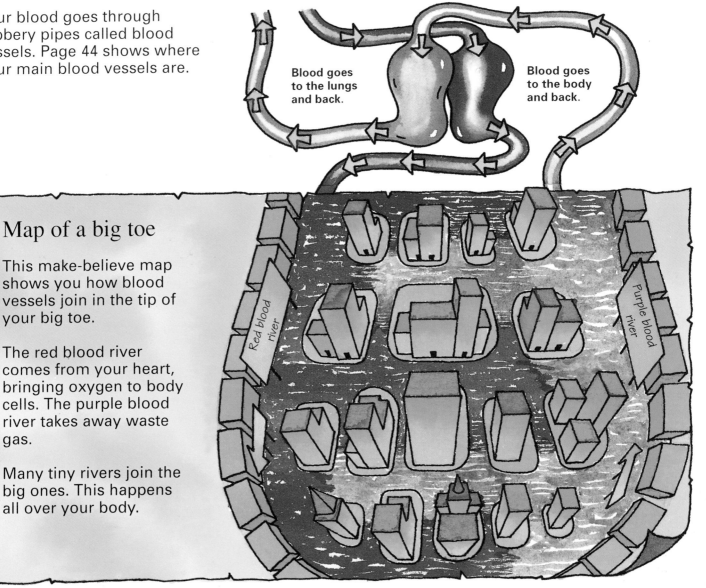

Blood goes to the lungs and back.

Blood goes to the body and back.

Map of a big toe

This make-believe map shows you how blood vessels join in the tip of your big toe.

The red blood river comes from your heart, bringing oxygen to body cells. The purple blood river takes away waste gas.

Many tiny rivers join the big ones. This happens all over your body.

Red blood river

Purple blood river

What makes your heart beat fast?

Your body has to make lots of energy when you run or dance or play football.

Your heart has to pump very hard and fast. It has to get lots of blood up to your lungs and back to get the oxygen your body needs to make energy.

Put your hand on your chest like this when you have been running. Feel how fast your heart is beating. You breathe more quickly too.

One-way blood system

There are many tiny gates inside the blood vessels going to your heart. They can only move one way, like trap doors. The blood can only go up – it cannot fall back.

See your blood vessels

Look in the mirror. Gently pull your lower eyelid down. Under it you will see red thready pieces. These are some of your tiniest blood vessels.

You have many tiny blood vessels. If you could join them all, end to end, they would stretch more than twice around the world.

How does blood get back to your heart?

ZZZ

WIGGLE

As you move around, your muscles help to move blood back to your heart. When you slow down your blood slows down as well.

If you wiggle your toes you can keep your feet from going to sleep. The working toe muscles help to speed the blood along.

Watch your blood move

The blue line on the inside of your wrist is blood. Rub your thumb up it like this. You will see the blood stop and then follow your thumb.

HOW YOU BREATHE

Your lungs are full of tiny holes, like sponges. They hang in your chest, in a space made by your ribs and a special muscle. When you breathe in, your chest swells up. Air fills your lungs like water in a sponge. This machine shows how it happens.

Air comes in.

Breathing in

To make you breathe in, your ribs swing up and out. The muscle under your lungs flattens down. Your lungs swell up, pulling air down your windpipe.

Ribs swing out.

Windpipe

Ribs

Lung

Muscle

Lungs swell up.

Muscle flattens down.

Your breathing machine

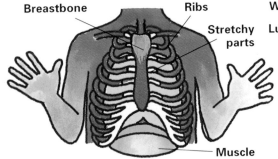

Breastbone

Ribs

Stretchy parts

Muscle

The muscle under your lungs is shaped like an upside-down saucer. When you breathe in, it flattens. Your ribs swell out, stretching the parts that join to your breastbone.

How your lungs look

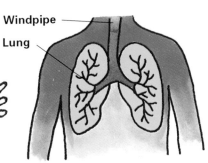

Windpipe

Lung

Your lungs are like sponges. They are made of tiny air sacs. Around each one is a net of blood vessels. They take oxygen from the air that you breathe in.

How much air?

2.5m (8ft) long

2.5m (8ft) wide

2.5m (8ft) high

Breathed-out air

Lots of air goes in and out of your lungs each day. If you could trap all the air that goes out of your lungs, it would fill a room as big as shown in the picture above.

Breathing out

When you breathe out, your ribs move back. The muscle under your ribs moves up again. Air is squeezed out of the tiny air sacs in your lungs.

Feel your ribs move

Cross your arms like this and take a deep breath. Can you feel your chest swell up? Tiny muscles criss-cross between your ribs. They make your ribs move out.

Air goes out.

Windpipe

Ribs fall back.

Ribs

Lung

Muscle

Air is squeezed out of lungs.

Muscle moves up.

Tummy breathing

The working muscle under your lungs pushes your stomach out and in. When ladies squeezed their waists with corsets, this muscle could not work. They often fainted.

Getting more lung power

If you sing, or play a musical instrument such as a trumpet, you need lots of lung power. You can learn to use the muscle under your lungs to get more lung power.

For practice, push the top of your stomach out as you breathe in. Hold your hand just under your chest, like the singer above, to feel it move. This fills your lungs really full.

A TALKING MACHINE

This machine does the main things that you do when you talk.

You tighten your vocal cords to make them vibrate when you breathe out. This makes sound waves – special ripples in the air. You use your teeth, tongue and mouth to turn the sound waves into words.

> The shape of your mouth helps to turn the sounds into words.

Tongue

Teeth

Lips

> The vibrating vocal cords make sound waves in the air.

Sound waves

> Your lips and tongue and teeth can break up or squeeze the sound to make it into words.

Vocal cords

Windpipe

> Your vocal cords are stretchy parts in your windpipe. You can tighten them. Then they vibrate as air pushes past them.

Your changing voice

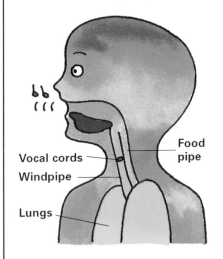

Vocal cords

Windpipe

Lungs

Food pipe

Your vocal cords become longer when you grow up. This makes your voice sound lower. A boy's vocal cords change more than a girl's.

> To make a sound you must let out air from your lungs. You use lots of air to make a loud sound.

14

Making words

The shape of your mouth changes to make different parts of words.

See how these people stretch and shape their mouths to make different sounds.

Watch yourself in the mirror while you talk. See how your own mouth changes shape.

Lip reading

You can sometimes understand what people are saying just by looking at the shape of their mouths as they speak.

Think how useful this might be if you were a spy.

Making sound waves

Blow up a balloon and let it go. The air rushing out will make the neck flap very fast. This is called vibration. It makes sound waves.

If you put a tube in the neck like this, there will be no sound as the air rushes out. The neck cannot vibrate and make sound waves.

Try stretching the neck to make high or low sounds. The wider you stretch the neck, the lower the sound. Your vocal cords work in a similar way.

WHAT EARS DO

Your ear is a machine that picks up sound waves and turns them into messages for your brain. We have invented a machine that might be able to do the things your ear does. Part of this machine sends messages about balance to your brain. Your ear does this, too.

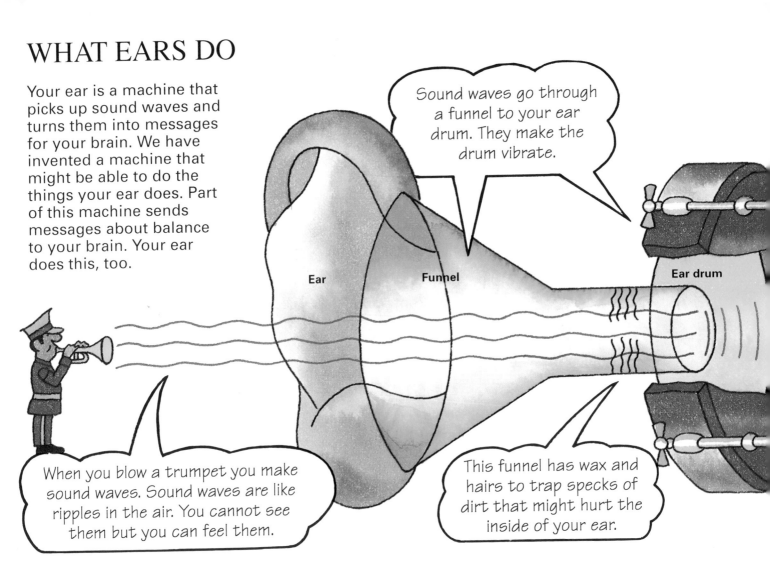

Sound waves go through a funnel to your ear drum. They make the drum vibrate.

Ear

Funnel

Ear drum

When you blow a trumpet you make sound waves. Sound waves are like ripples in the air. You cannot see them but you can feel them.

This funnel has wax and hairs to trap specks of dirt that might hurt the inside of your ear.

Your ear machinery

Your inner ear is a curled-up tube with three loops attached. The liquid in the curled-up part picks up sound waves. The loops are to help you keep your balance (see opposite).

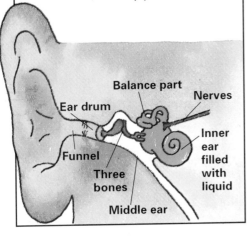

Balance part

Nerves

Ear drum

Funnel

Three bones

Middle ear

Inner ear filled with liquid

Feeling sound waves

Hold a cardboard tube against a balloon, as shown below, and speak into it. The sound waves will make the balloon vibrate. You can feel this with your fingers.

Only one ear

You need both ears in order to know where sounds are coming from. Try this. Turn on the radio. Cover your eyes, cover up one ear, and turn around a few times. Where is the radio?

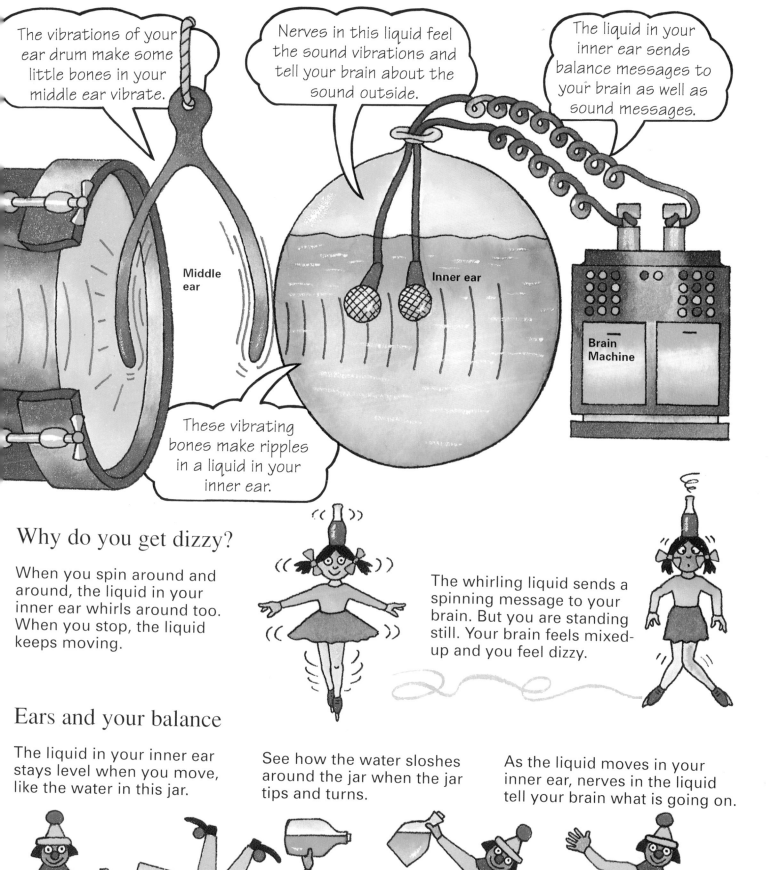

The vibrations of your ear drum make some little bones in your middle ear vibrate.

Nerves in this liquid feel the sound vibrations and tell your brain about the sound outside.

The liquid in your inner ear sends balance messages to your brain as well as sound messages.

Middle ear

Inner ear

These vibrating bones make ripples in a liquid in your inner ear.

Brain Machine

Why do you get dizzy?

When you spin around and around, the liquid in your inner ear whirls around too. When you stop, the liquid keeps moving.

The whirling liquid sends a spinning message to your brain. But you are standing still. Your brain feels mixed-up and you feel dizzy.

Ears and your balance

The liquid in your inner ear stays level when you move, like the water in this jar.

See how the water sloshes around the jar when the jar tips and turns.

As the liquid moves in your inner ear, nerves in the liquid tell your brain what is going on.

17

HOW AN EYE WORKS

Your eye is like a camera. A camera takes in light rays from the outside world and squeezes them to fit on a small piece of film. Your eyes gather light rays into a very tiny picture that fits onto the back of your eyeball. A nerve from this spot sends the picture to your brain.

On the right is a machine we invented to show the important parts of your eye and what each part does.

> Light rays from the spotlight bounce off the clown and make it possible to see him.

Light rays

Light rays

> Light rays from the clown go through this lens (the cornea). The lens bends the light rays.

A picture of an eye

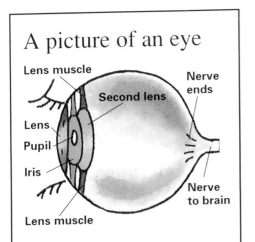

Lens muscle

Second lens

Nerve ends

Lens

Pupil

Iris

Nerve to brain

Lens muscle

This picture shows where the different parts of your eye are. You can also see the muscles that change the shape of the lens in your eye.

What a lens does

A magnifying glass is a lens. You can make it bend light rays into an upside-down picture. Try this.

Hold a magnifying glass between a flashlight and some white paper. Move the glass back and forth until you can see a clear pattern of light on the paper. You may have to move the paper.

Now hold your thumb over the flashlight, at the top, like this.

Where is your thumb in the pattern on the paper?

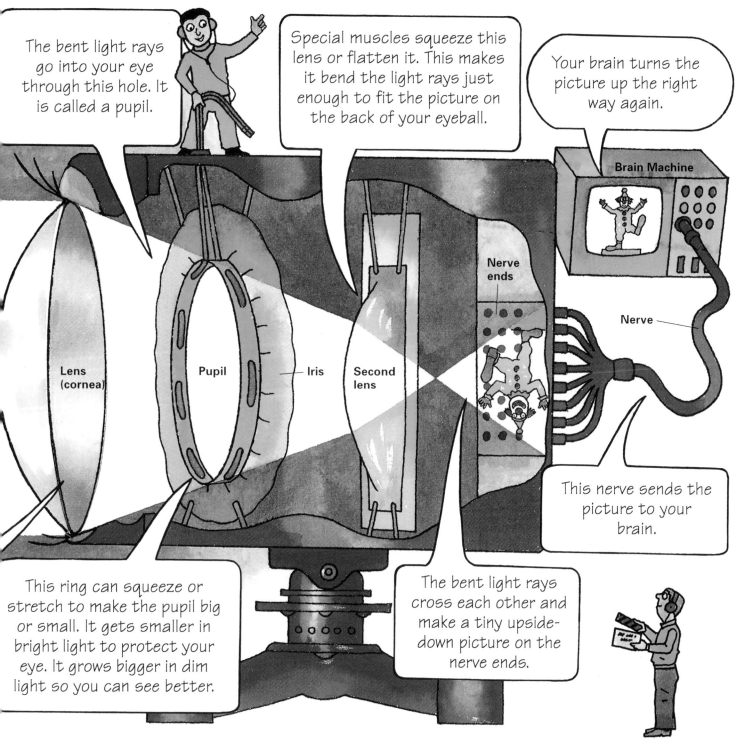

Watch your pupil shrink

How your pupil shrinks

Look in a mirror. Close your eyes nearly shut. Your pupils will get bigger.

Now open your eyes quickly. Watch carefully and you will see your pupils shrinking.

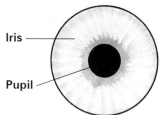

The ring around your pupil is called the iris. If you look closely, you can see the muscles in it that make the pupil bigger or smaller.

HOW TWO EYES WORK TOGETHER

Each of your eyes sees a slightly different picture of the world. Your brain puts the two pictures together. On this page you can see how the picture changes in your brain.

When you look at something close, it is easy to notice the difference in what your two eyes see. Just try this trick:

See-through pencil

Print a word in large letters on some paper. Hold a pencil halfway between your eyes and the paper. If you close either eye, part of the word will be hidden. But if you stare hard at the paper with both eyes, you will see the whole word.

Why do you have two eyes?

Close one eye. Hold a pencil in one hand. Stretch out your arm as shown above and try to touch something. Can you do it? Two eyes working together help you to see how close things are.

The brain puts the two pictures together.

Brain Machine

The left eye can see an extra piece of the left side.

The right eye can see an extra piece of the right side.

Left eye

Right eye

WHAT NOSES DO

This picture shows you how your nose cleans and warms the air you breathe.

The air is full of germs and tiny specks of dirt. We have made them into bugs so you can see how they get trapped.

A special gas floats away from things that have a smell. We have made it look like stars to show what happens to it.

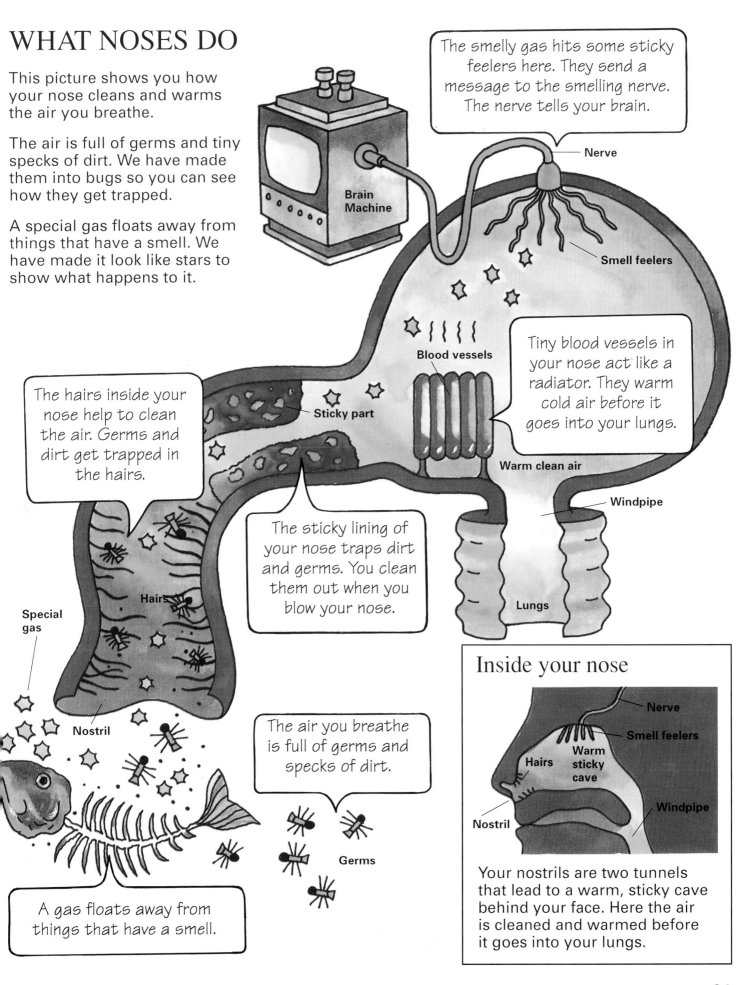

The smelly gas hits some sticky feelers here. They send a message to the smelling nerve. The nerve tells your brain.

Brain Machine

Nerve

Smell feelers

Blood vessels

Tiny blood vessels in your nose act like a radiator. They warm cold air before it goes into your lungs.

Sticky part

Warm clean air

Windpipe

The hairs inside your nose help to clean the air. Germs and dirt get trapped in the hairs.

The sticky lining of your nose traps dirt and germs. You clean them out when you blow your nose.

Lungs

Hairs

Special gas

Nostril

The air you breathe is full of germs and specks of dirt.

Germs

A gas floats away from things that have a smell.

Inside your nose

Nerve

Smell feelers

Warm sticky cave

Hairs

Windpipe

Nostril

Your nostrils are two tunnels that lead to a warm, sticky cave behind your face. Here the air is cleaned and warmed before it goes into your lungs.

A FEELING MACHINE

Tiny nerves in your skin tell you if things are hot or cold, hard or smooth. Your fingers have many nerves. You use them a lot for finding out about things.

This machine explores the world, like your fingers do. Its feelers act like the nerves in your skin. Each kind of feeler tests for something special.

This feeler tests for coldness.

The brain gets messages from all these feelers.

These feelers test for smoothness or roughness. They pick up light and gentle touches.

This feeler tests the heat of things.

This pressure feeler sends messages about bumps. It presses things to test for hardness.

Any feeling that is too strong - like a hard bump or too much heat - becomes a pain message. It tells your brain that something is hurting you.

22

TOUCHING, FEELING, FINDING OUT

Your brain gets messages about feelings from nerves in your skin and nerves all through your body. These messages fool your brain sometimes. Read on and see why this happens.

The next four pages show how your brain sorts out all the messages that come from the different parts of your body.

Mysterious pains

Tiny hurts on places like your feet or your tongue can feel enormous. Why?

These places are crowded with feeling nerves. Your brain gets lots of messages – but they all come from the same spot.

Feely box trick

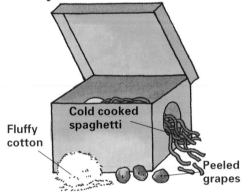

For this trick you need a box with two hand-holes and some things that feel funny.

Put the things inside, one by one, through one hole. Get your friends to stick their hands through the other hole and guess what is inside.

Itchy back problems

The nerves on your back are far apart. A big space may contain only one nerve so it can be hard to tell exactly where a tickle itches.

Your muscle nerves

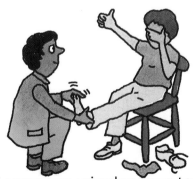

If someone wiggles your toe, you can tell without looking whether the toe is up or down. You get messages from feeling nerves in your muscles.

Why do you have pains?

Nerves inside your body tell when something is hurting inside you. This helps people to know what to do when you are ill.

Back feeler trick

Touch someone's back with a pencil. Then touch with two pencils at once. If the pencils are closer than 2cm (1in), he may think there is still only one.

WHAT HAPPENS IN YOUR BRAIN

Your brain is a little like a busy telephone system that receives and sends out lots of messages. We made up this machine to show how the messages go through the main parts of your brain.

Your five senses

Your senses bring messages about the world around you. Your memory helps you to understand what the messages mean.

Hearing

Your ear hears this noise. Your memory says, "Car!"

Sight

Your eyes see this. Your memory says, "Watch out!"

Smell

Your nose smells this. Your memory says, "It might be a cake!"

Taste

Your tongue says sour. Your memory says, "Not ripe!"

Touch

The skin on your fingers feels hair. Your memory helps you to decide who it is.

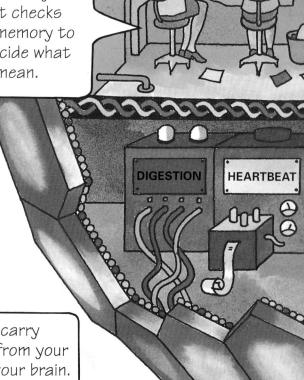

This part gets important news from your senses. This helps it to decide plans for action. It can shut out some messages that are not important.

This part gets lots of messages from your senses. It checks with your memory to help to decide what they mean.

Nerves carry messages from your senses to your brain.

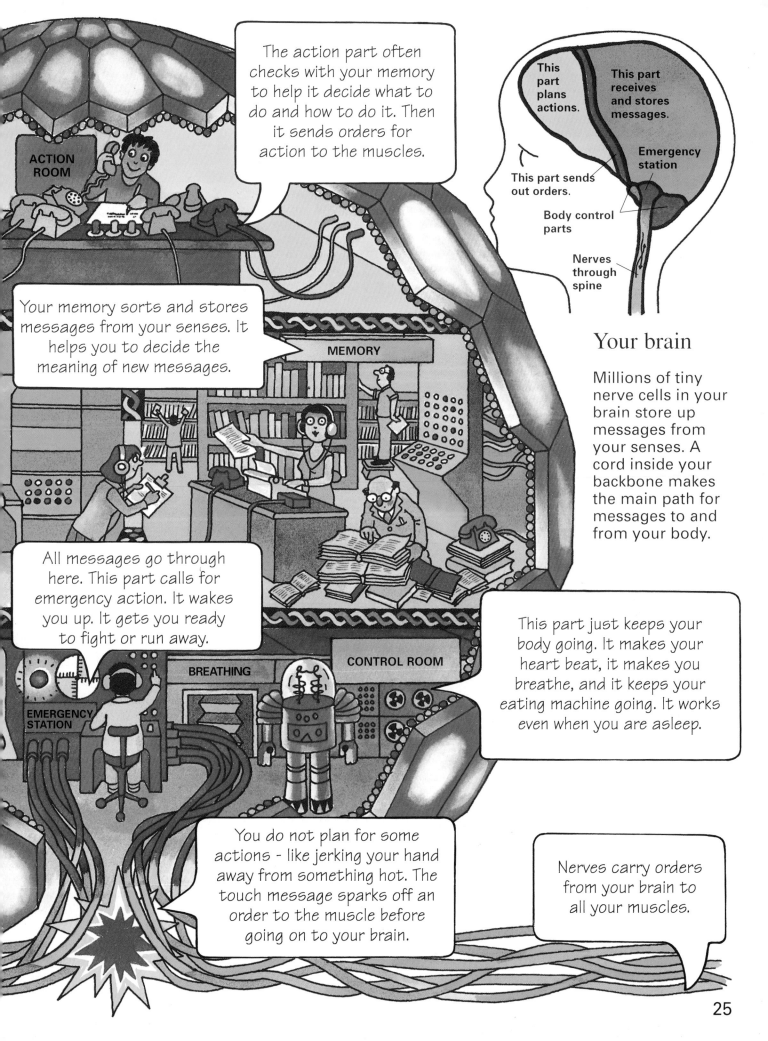

The action part often checks with your memory to help it decide what to do and how to do it. Then it sends orders for action to the muscles.

ACTION ROOM

This part plans actions.

This part receives and stores messages.

This part sends out orders.

Emergency station

Body control parts

Nerves through spine

Your memory sorts and stores messages from your senses. It helps you to decide the meaning of new messages.

MEMORY

Your brain

Millions of tiny nerve cells in your brain store up messages from your senses. A cord inside your backbone makes the main path for messages to and from your body.

All messages go through here. This part calls for emergency action. It wakes you up. It gets you ready to fight or run away.

EMERGENCY STATION

BREATHING

CONTROL ROOM

This part just keeps your body going. It makes your heart beat, it makes you breathe, and it keeps your eating machine going. It works even when you are asleep.

You do not plan for some actions - like jerking your hand away from something hot. The touch message sparks off an order to the muscle before going on to your brain.

Nerves carry orders from your brain to all your muscles.

ALARM... a story of your brain in action

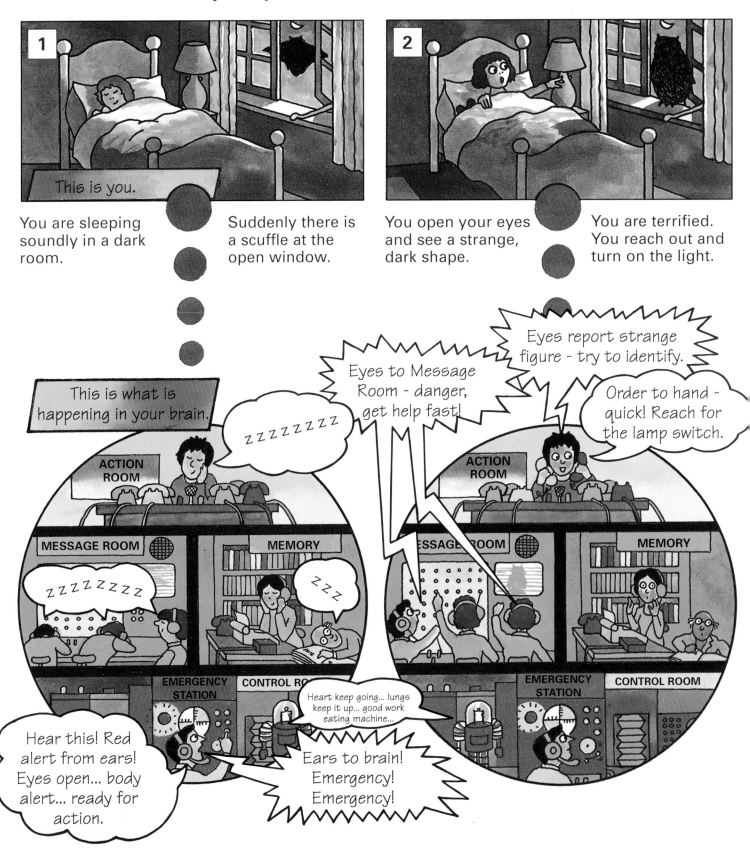

You are sleeping soundly in a dark room.

Suddenly there is a scuffle at the open window.

You open your eyes and see a strange, dark shape.

You are terrified. You reach out and turn on the light.

Most of the brain is resting but the control room is always busy. And the emergency station is always ready for action.

Now the newsroom can find out more about the strange noise. The action part can get the body's muscles going.

Oh, it's only the owl that lives in the tree outside.

He gives a hoot to prove it, before he flies away.

You turn off the light and go back to sleep again.

Here the brain is using messages from many senses to decide what is happening. It uses memories, too.

The emergency is over. Most of the brain shuts down. The emergency station will take over now, to watch over the body while it sleeps.

HOW BONES FIT TOGETHER

The places where your bones link are called joints. The big made-up skeleton on these two pages shows how your main joints work. The picture on the right shows a real skeleton.

You use your knee and elbow joints a lot. Try going stiff-legged and stiff-armed for half an hour. Can you eat or throw a ball? Can you run or climb stairs?

Many little joints in your feet and ankles move when you run. Try to run on your heels and feel the difference.

Muscles join the parts that stick out on your backbone. Bendy pads made of a substance called cartilage make cushions between each two bones.

Elbow joint

Knee joint

Parts that stick out on your backbone

Robot skeleton

This made-up skeleton will not work as well as yours. Its metal pieces will be hard to move. Real bone is light. It is full of tiny holes, like honeycomb.

Your body makes a special liquid that oils your joints. Otherwise you might creak.

Oil

The little bones in your ankles and wrists let you make small, quick movements. The ends of the bones slide across each other.

Special covers help to hold joints together and keep in the oily liquid.

Ligaments

Tough straps called ligaments hold the joints in place.

Special cover

Your elbows and knees are special types of hinge joints. They can move in more ways than the joints in your fingers.

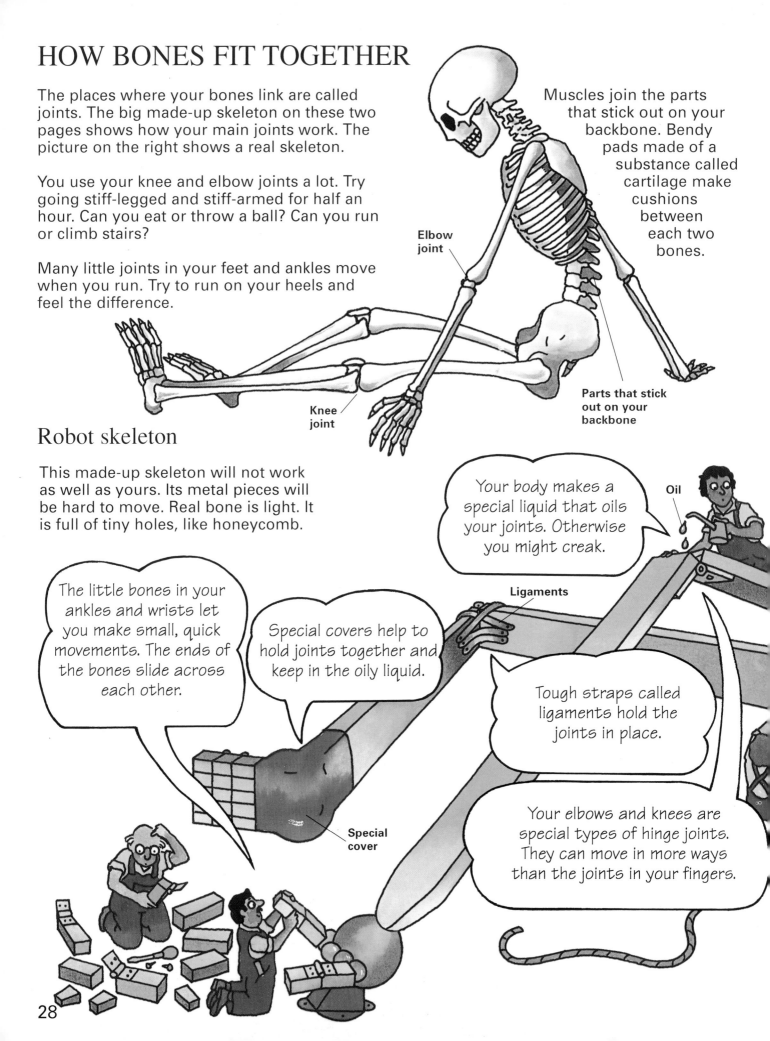

28

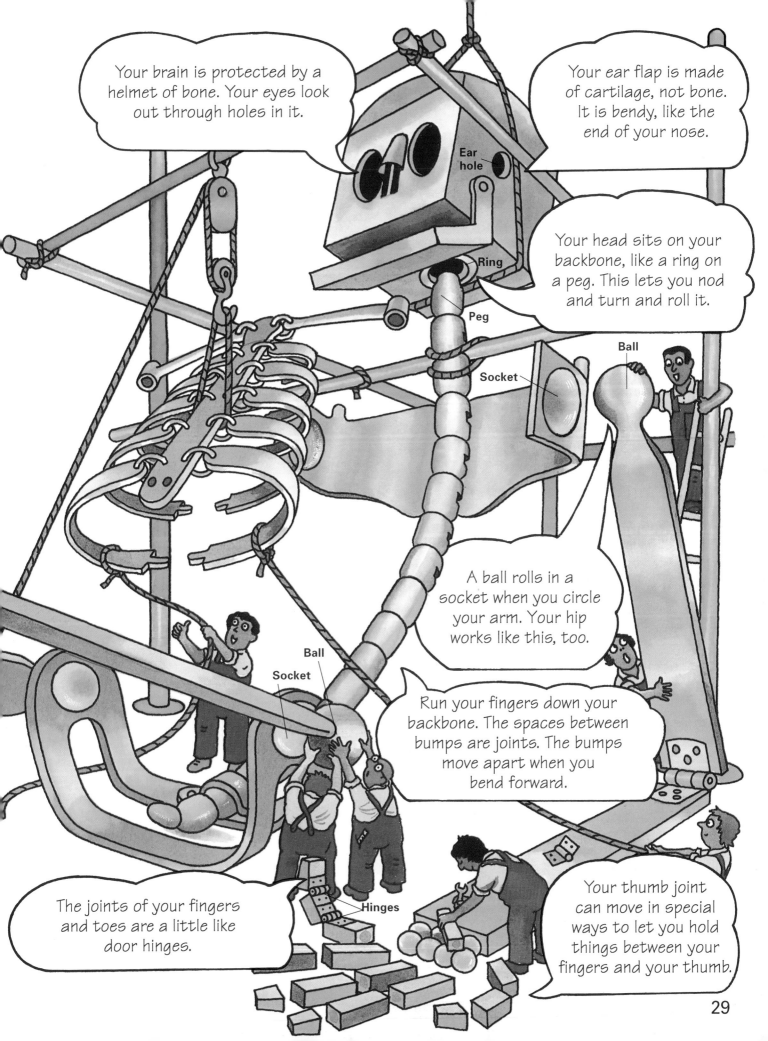

29

HOW MUSCLES WORK

The springs on this made-up skeleton work like muscles. Look to see how they join the movable parts. They work these parts the way your muscles work your bones. Nerves connect these muscles to your brain. Messages from your brain make them work.

Your brain can send many messages and work many muscles at the same time. Other muscles work things inside you, such as your heart and eating machinery. A special part of your brain keeps these muscles under control.

Working in pairs

Each joint is worked by two muscles. They work in turn, as shown on the right. You can feel the muscles that work your wrist by holding your arm below your elbow and wiggling your wrist. You can feel these muscles bulge in turn.

Bend your wrist.

Straighten your wrist.

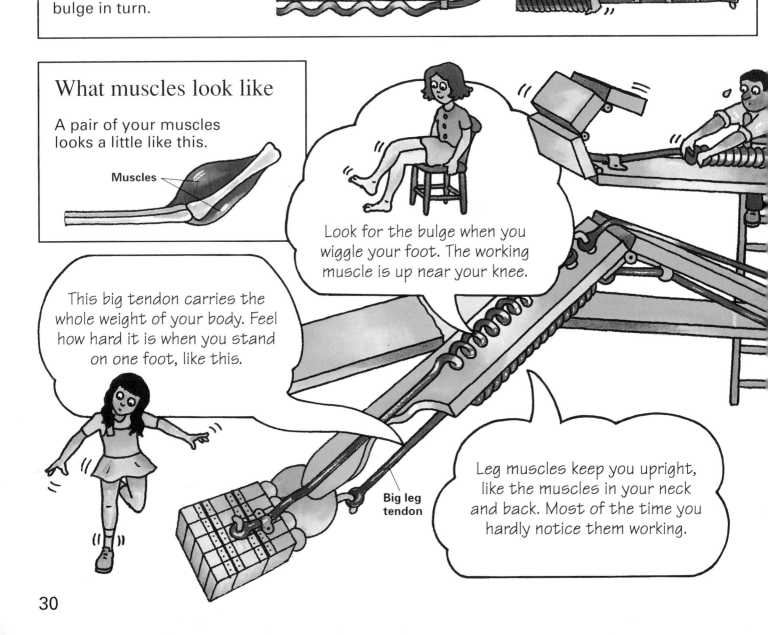

What muscles look like

A pair of your muscles looks a little like this.

Muscles

Look for the bulge when you wiggle your foot. The working muscle is up near your knee.

This big tendon carries the whole weight of your body. Feel how hard it is when you stand on one foot, like this.

Big leg tendon

Leg muscles keep you upright, like the muscles in your neck and back. Most of the time you hardly notice them working.

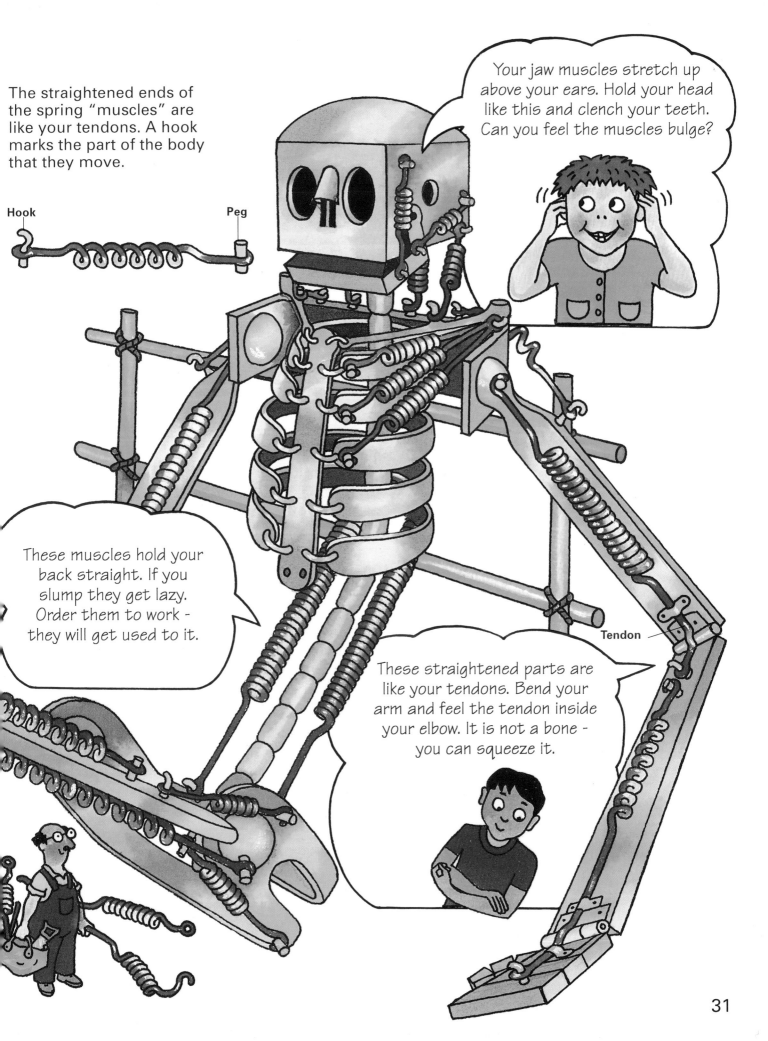

WHAT SKIN DOES

All over your body is a coat of skin. You can only see the surface of it. On this page we have made a huge picture of a piece of skin to show what happens underneath.

The skin that you see on the surface is a layer of dead pieces. This layer is dry, tough and waterproof. It protects your body from germs and from drying up.

Just under it is a second layer where new skin is made. Parts in this layer are fed by blood vessels in the deep layer. The parts die as they get pushed to the surface.

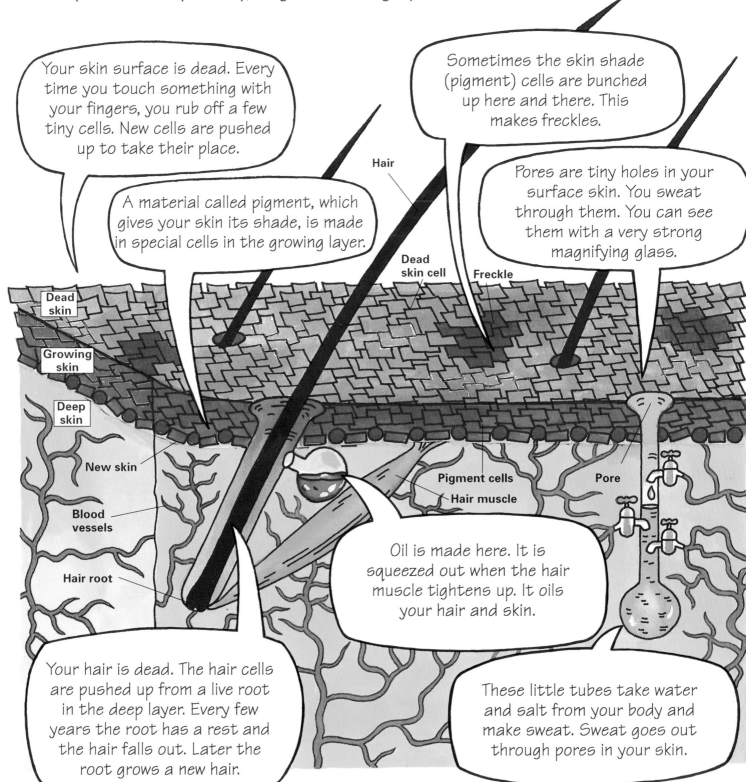

Your skin surface is dead. Every time you touch something with your fingers, you rub off a few tiny cells. New cells are pushed up to take their place.

A material called pigment, which gives your skin its shade, is made in special cells in the growing layer.

Sometimes the skin shade (pigment) cells are bunched up here and there. This makes freckles.

Pores are tiny holes in your surface skin. You sweat through them. You can see them with a very strong magnifying glass.

Hair

Dead skin cell

Freckle

Dead skin

Growing skin

Deep skin

New skin

Blood vessels

Hair root

Pigment cells

Hair muscle

Pore

Oil is made here. It is squeezed out when the hair muscle tightens up. It oils your hair and skin.

Your hair is dead. The hair cells are pushed up from a live root in the deep layer. Every few years the root has a rest and the hair falls out. Later the root grows a new hair.

These little tubes take water and salt from your body and make sweat. Sweat goes out through pores in your skin.

If you had no skin...

Your body is made mostly of water. There is even some water in your bones. If you had no skin, the sun and air would dry you up like a prune.

Waterproof skin

Your skin makes oil which helps to keep the surface waterproof. Water does not soak into your skin. You can rub it off with a towel.

Why should you wash?

Dirt and dust from the air stick to the oil made by your skin. You have to use soap and warm water to wash off the dirty oil.

When it is hot and sunny

Sweat

Tan

When you are hot, the sweat glands make more sweat. The sweat goes out through pores in your skin. As it dries, it cools down your skin.

Your blood takes heat from your body. When you are hot, more blood moves through the vessels near the skin's surface. Then the air cools it.

Sunlight makes the skin's pigment cells turn darker. Some of the sun's rays are bad for you. Dark skin protects your body from the harmful rays.

When it is cold

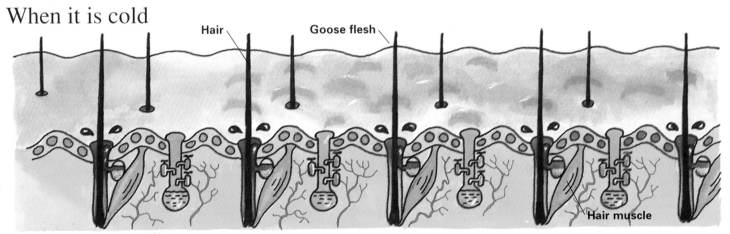

Hair

Goose flesh

Hair muscle

The air takes heat from your skin. When it is cold the blood vessels squeeze down in your skin to keep the warmth in. This makes you look paler.

Cold makes your hair muscles tighten. Then your hair stands up. On furry animals, hair traps a blanket of warm air. This helps to keep them warm.

When a hair muscle tightens, it gets short and fat. This squeezes out oil, makes your hair stand up, and makes goose flesh on your skin.

33

HOW BODIES FIGHT GERMS

Your body is always being attacked by germs. But it is well defended, like the castle in this picture. Your skin makes a strong barrier – like a castle wall.

Germs cannot get through healthy skin. If skin is hurt, cells in the blood help to heal it and fight off the germs. They act like the warriors shown in the picture.

Germs can get into your body through openings such as your mouth and your nose. But each of these openings is protected in some way. There are also ways you can help your body to defend itself. Look around this picture and see what they are.

> Tears kill germs. When you blink, tears wash your eyes.

> Your nose has sticky hairs that trap germs in the air you breathe.

> Saliva (spit) washes germs down into your stomach. Stomach juices can kill most germs.

> Your mouth is an easy place for germs to get in. Be careful what you put into it.

Saliva (spit)

Germ army

What are germs?

Germs are tiny creatures, too small to see. If they get into your body they make you ill. They make poisons. They become powerful armies.

Germs like warm, dark, dirty places. Sun and fresh air kill them. Soapy water kills them. Good food helps your body to make weapons to fight them.

Why you have injections

Some germs have secret weapons. If a lot of them made a surprise attack you would be very ill. So the doctor shoots some weak germs into you.

Needle

Your ear hole has wax and hairs to trap germs.

Special white cells in your blood fight germs. Different kinds do different jobs. Some of them corner the germs and others kill them.

Your blood is always moving around your body. When germs attack, your blood carries the messages for help. Then lots of fighting white cells come.

Red blood cells

White blood cell

Repair cells make a net and other cells bunch up behind it. Then blood cannot run out and germs cannot get in.

Ear hole

Sweat pores

Cut

Your blood has special repair cells. When you are cut they make some sticky stuff that turns tiny pieces in your blood into a net.

Tiny holes called pores let out sweat. Clean sweat kills germs. But old sweat traps dirt - so wash it off.

What is a scab?

Your blood cells learn about the new weapons from the weak germs, and decide how to destroy them. Then you are prepared for an attack.

Part of your blood makes a net when you are cut. Your blood cells bunch up behind it. This makes a blood clot. Dried clotted blood becomes a scab.

The scab protects your body while new skin is being built underneath it. When the new skin is ready, the scab falls off.

35

SHOPPING TRIP GAME

On the opposite page are pictures of seven important kinds of food. You need a little of each kind every few days to stay really fit and healthy.

Play this game for some practice in choosing the right kinds of food. The object of the game is to get some of each of the seven important kinds of food before you reach Home. Make a score card like the one shown below. Mark it each time you land on a food square. The winner is the first player Home with the Big Seven.

Sweet things take up room needed for important things. If you score more than one of these, you must return to the start.

Rules

Each player needs a counter, a pencil and a score card. Throw a dice to see how many places you can move. Mark your score card every time you land on a food square.

If you collect two sweet things, cross out both and return to the start.

If you get Home without the Big Seven, return to the start.

You may use your turn to change places with another player. He does not lose his next turn.

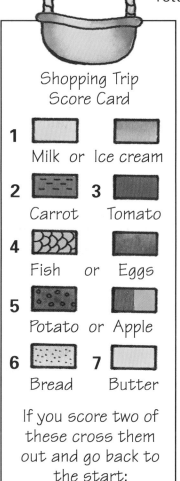

Shopping Trip
Score Card

1 Milk or Ice cream

2 Carrot   3 Tomato

4 Fish or Eggs

5 Potato or Apple

6 Bread   7 Butter

If you score two of these cross them out and go back to the start:

Chocolate bar   Cream cakes

Sugary drink

1 Score fish.

2 Score eggs.

3 Score butter and milk.

14 Score potatoes.

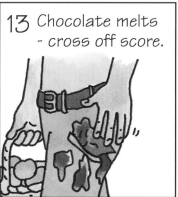

13 Chocolate melts - cross off score.

12 Score sugary drink.

15 Score bread.

16 Score cream cakes.

17 Gone bad - cross out one potato score.

Food groups

1

Milk and cheese for strong bones and healthy teeth.

2

Leafy green and yellow vegetables for shiny hair and good skin.

3

Tomatoes, oranges and lemons to fight germs, such as cold germs.

4

Meat, fish and eggs for good muscle.

5
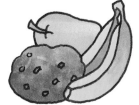
These vegetables and fruit help in general.

6

Brown bread and cereals for energy.

7

Butter for healthy skin and hair.

4 Score ice cream.

5 Eggs broken - cross out one egg score.

6 Ice cream melts - cross out score.

7 Score chocolate bar.

11 Fish lost - cross out one fish score.

10 Score tomatoes.

9 Score apples.

8 Score carrots.

18 Drop cream cakes - cross off score.

19 Apple has worm - cross out one apple score.

20 Squashed - cross out one tomato score.

HOME

HOW A BABY STARTS

A baby starts when two special cells meet – a sperm cell from a man's body and an egg cell from a woman's body. Joined inside the woman's body, these two cells grow into a whole new person.

Men and women each have special parts for making these cells and helping them to join. We made up these Mother and Father Machines to show how they work.

The Father Machine

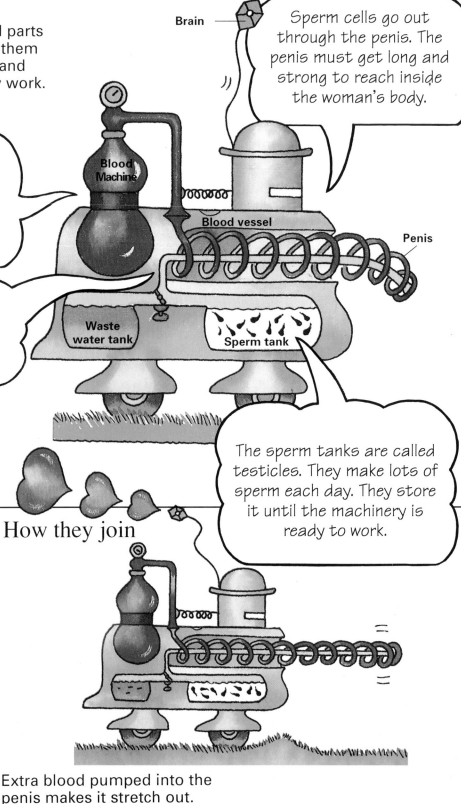

Sperm cells go out through the penis. The penis must get long and strong to reach inside the woman's body.

At special times, extra blood is pumped into the spongy walls of the penis. This makes it long and hard. The pictures below show this.

Sperm and waste water go out through the same pipe. A tiny gate shuts off the waste water while sperm goes through.

The sperm tanks are called testicles. They make lots of sperm each day. They store it until the machinery is ready to work.

Brain
Blood Machine
Blood vessel
Penis
Waste water tank
Sperm tank

A boy's special parts

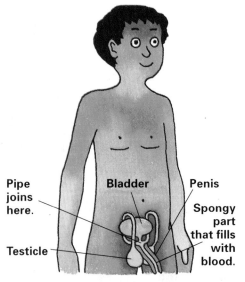

Pipe joins here.
Bladder
Penis
Spongy part that fills with blood.
Testicle

A boy's testicles are his sperm tanks. They start working usually between the ages of 10 and 18. The sperm pipes join the pipe that takes waste water from his bladder.

How they join

Extra blood pumped into the penis makes it stretch out.

The Mother Machine

Thousands of tiny egg cells are stored in here. Every four weeks, one egg slips down to the uterus.

This stretchy tunnel joins the uterus to the special opening in the woman's body.

Brain

Ovary

Vagina

Special opening

Cushiony lining

Egg

Uterus

The uterus grows a sort of cushiony lining for each egg.

A girl's special parts

Ovaries

Uterus

Vagina

Special opening between legs.

A girl is born with thousands of tiny egg cells in her body. When she is between about 10 and 17 they start to travel one by one into her uterus. It makes a sort of cushion for each egg.

Unless a baby starts, the uterus clears everything out once a month to get ready for a new egg.

The vagina gets soft and stretchy. This makes it easy for the penis to fit in.

Muscles squeeze the sperm pipe to shoot sperm far inside. They are on their way to meet the egg. Turn the page to see what happens next.

HOW A BABY IS BORN

These pictures show the main things that happen as a baby grows in its mother and as it is born.

The baby's story

No one knows yet that a baby has started.

The baby is just a dot inside the mother.

Before the start...

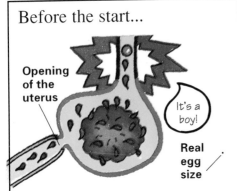

Opening of the uterus

It's a boy!

Real egg size

First, sperm swim up to meet the egg. A sperm is much smaller than an egg. It has the message that decides whether a boy or girl is made.

At the beginning...

The egg is joined by just one sperm. It grows by splitting into more cells which quickly grow and split again. The growing egg nestles into the lining of the uterus.

At one month...

Water bag

The cluster of cells is about the size of a small bean. It has grown a water bag around itself. The growing baby floats inside, warm and safe.

The mother's bosom is bigger now. It is getting ready to make milk for the baby.

When the muscles squeeze, she knows the baby will soon be born.

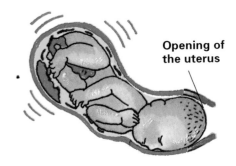

The muscles squeeze and squeeze. This is hard work.

At nine months...

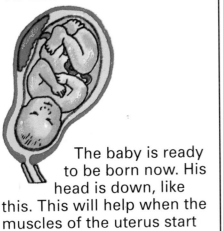

The baby is ready to be born now. His head is down, like this. This will help when the muscles of the uterus start to push him out.

At the start of birth...

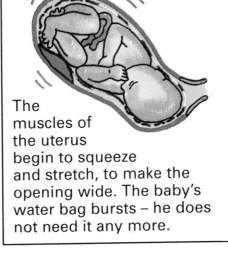

The muscles of the uterus begin to squeeze and stretch, to make the opening wide. The baby's water bag bursts – he does not need it any more.

Opening of the uterus

The muscles have worked for hours now. See how wide the opening of the uterus is. The baby's head is pressing against it – this helps it to open.

Now the mother knows a baby has started – her uterus has kept its special lining.

At two months...

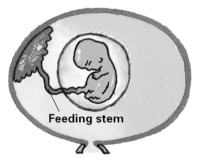

Now the baby looks a bit like this. It grows on a sort of stem. Food and oxygen from the blood in the lining of the uterus go through the stem to the baby.

Feeding stem

By this time she can feel a small bump where the baby is growing.

At four months...

The little buds on the bean shape have grown into arms and legs. The cluster of cells is a complete baby. But he is still too weak to live in the outside world.

Sometimes she can feel the baby kick.

At five months...

The baby grows bigger and stronger every day. He can move around now – he even kicks sometimes. The doctor can hear his heart beating.

Now the mother works very hard helping to push the baby down and out.

Now the muscles of the uterus begin to squeeze very hard. They push the baby's head right through the opening of the uterus.

Then the baby slides out through the mother's vagina. This little tunnel can stretch very wide for the baby to go through.

Born!

The baby is born. His feeding stem is snipped and tied – his own lungs and eating machinery will do that work now. The knot becomes a belly button, just like yours.

HOW YOUR BODY FITS TOGETHER

These pictures show some of the main parts of your body. You could trace the skeleton and place it over the other pictures to see how your bones fit your breathing and eating machinery.

Pictures on the next pages show your main nerves and blood vessels. The skeleton fits these pictures too.

Your breathing machine

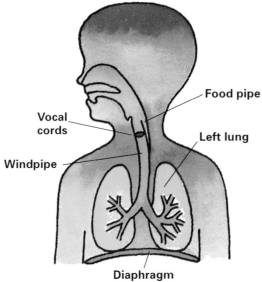

Food pipe

Vocal cords

Windpipe

Left lung

Diaphragm

Your lungs hang in the space made by your ribs and a muscle called the diaphragm.

Your skeleton

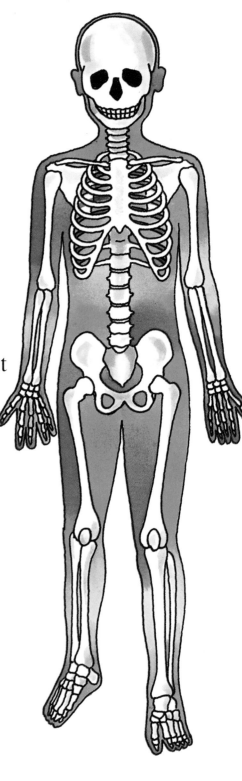

There are more than 200 bones in your body.

Your eating machine

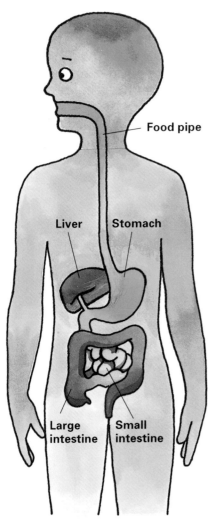

Food pipe

Liver

Stomach

Large intestine

Small intestine

Fine thready pieces hold your intestines to your backbone. The tummy and back muscles help to protect them.

How waste water gets out

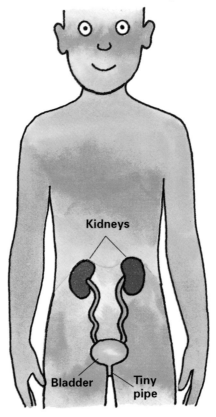

Kidneys

Bladder

Tiny pipe

Waste water stored in your bladder goes out through a tiny pipe. A boy's pipe is longer than a girl's.

Important front muscles   Important back muscles   What muscles look like

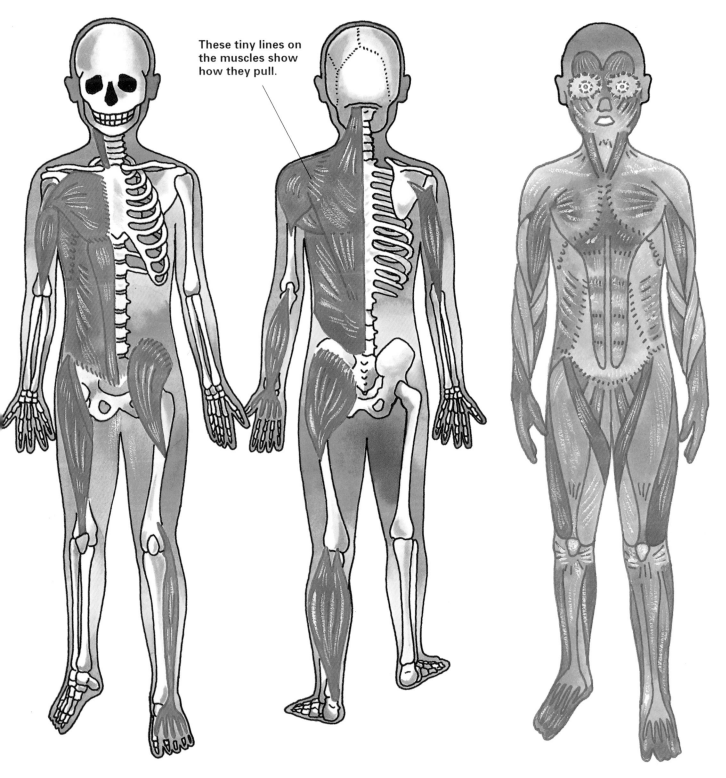

These tiny lines on the muscles show how they pull.

These are some of the main muscles that join the front of your skeleton.

This picture shows some of the big muscles that join the back of your skeleton.

Hundreds of muscles weave together like this to make the fleshy cover of your body.

Your main blood vessels

Your main nerves

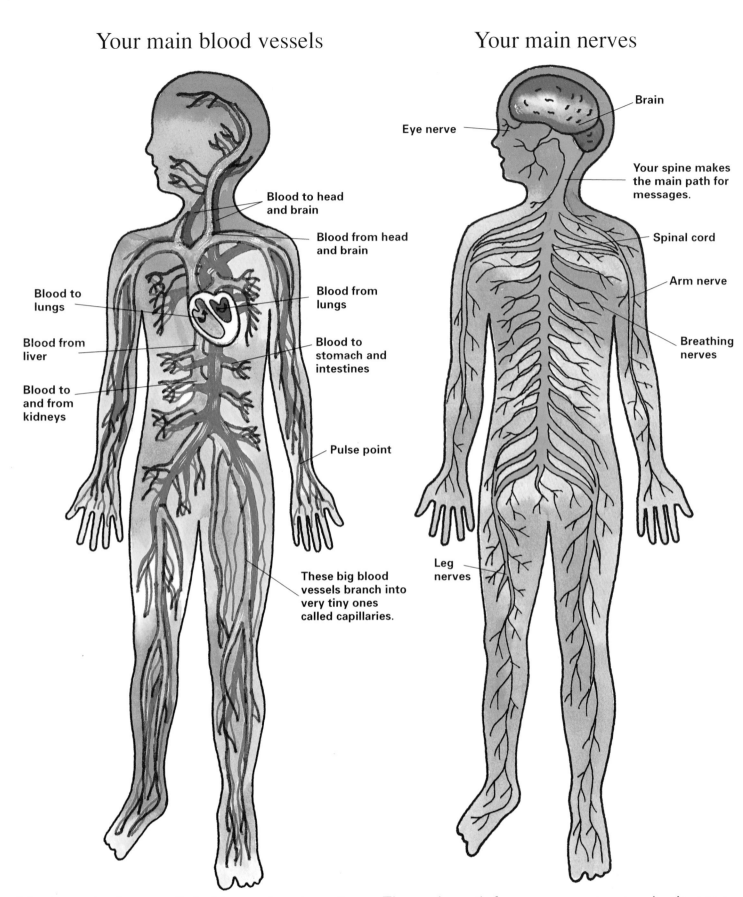

Blood to head and brain

Blood from head and brain

Blood to lungs

Blood from lungs

Blood from liver

Blood to stomach and intestines

Blood to and from kidneys

Pulse point

These big blood vessels branch into very tiny ones called capillaries.

Eye nerve

Brain

Your spine makes the main path for messages.

Spinal cord

Arm nerve

Breathing nerves

Leg nerves

The heart is shown a little bigger than it really is, so you can see how the blood goes through it. The blood vessels leading out are called arteries. The ones leading in are called veins.

The main path for messages to your brain goes right through the middle of your backbone. The main nerves connect to it like this. Hundreds of tiny nerves join these big ones.

WHAT ARE BODIES MADE OF?

Your body, like all living things, is made of very tiny parts called cells. You have many kinds of cells. Each does a different kind of work. Here are some of them.

Groups of the same kind of cell are called tissue. The different parts of your body are made of different kinds of body tissue.

How big is a cell?

Most cells are so very small that you would need a very strong microscope to see them. Try this to see how small they are:

Peel off one of the layers of thick skin on an onion. Under it you will find a sort of thin tissue. This is just one cell thick. Feel it. It is so thin you can see through it.

A muscle cell	Muscle tissue	A muscle

This is a muscle cell. It can squeeze and stretch.	Muscle cells join into stringy pieces called fibres. You can see this muscle tissue in meat.	A muscle squeezes when all of its cells squeeze.

Nerve cell

A bundle of nerve cells

The long bits pick up and carry messages.

Nerve cells join together into bundles, like wires in a telephone cable.

These bundles of nerves join the main cable in your spine that goes to your brain.

Red blood cells

Red blood cells going through blood vessels

A drop of blood under a microscope shows cells floating in a clear liquid.

Red blood cells carry oxygen to other body cells. The liquid part of your blood carries food.

All of your cells need food and oxygen to stay alive and do their work.

Skin cells

Stages of skin cell growth

Only the bottom layer of cells is alive. It makes new cells and pushes them up.

This picture shows how a new cell is made. The growing skin cell is shown in red.

See how the cell swells and stretches until it breaks into two cells.

BODY WORDS

Eating words

Abdomen The part of your body under your chest where your stomach and intestines are found.
Anus The hole where solid waste goes out of your body.
Bladder The bag that stores waste water.
Carbohydrates Foods such as bread and potatoes that give you energy.
Epiglottis A flap of cartilage behind your tongue which stops food going down your windpipe.
Faeces Undigested food (solid waste) that goes out of your body through your anus.
Fats Foods such as butter and oil that give you energy.
Oesophagus The food pipe that goes to your stomach.
Proteins Foods such as meat, eggs and cheese that make muscle.
Urine A mixture of water and waste taken from your blood by your kidneys. It is stored in your bladder until it goes out of your body.
Vitamins Important things in food that keep you healthy.

Breathing words

Bronchial tubes The tubes that lead from your windpipe to your lungs.
Diaphragm The sheet of muscle between your lungs and your stomach that helps you to breathe.
Larynx The part of your windpipe that holds your vocal cords.
Lungs The two air bags in your chest you use for breathing.
Trachea Your windpipe.

Blood and heart words

Antibody A special weapon made by the blood to fight germs.
Artery A blood vessel that takes blood from your heart to elsewhere in your body.
Blood vessel A tube that carries blood.
Capillary A very tiny blood vessel that brings supplies to the cells and takes away waste.
Plasma The watery, liquid part of the blood.
Vein A blood vessel that carries blood to your heart from elsewhere in your body.

Bone, muscle and skin words

Cartilage Gristle, which is a bit like bendy bone.
Joint Where two bones link.
Spine Your backbone.
Tendon A tough, stringy piece that connects muscle to bone.
Vertebra One of the bones that make up your backbone.

Baby-making words

Fertilization The joining of an egg and a sperm to start making a baby.
Menstruation The clearing out of the uterus each month if a baby does not start.
Ovary The part of a girl's body that stores eggs.
Ovum The egg cell in a girl's body that becomes a baby when it is fertilized.

Penis The part of a boy that lets out urine and sperm.
Placenta The cushiony lining of the uterus that brings food to an unborn baby and takes away waste.
Puberty The time when the baby-making machinery starts working in a girl or boy.
Sperm The special cells made by a boy's testicles that can fertilize girl's egg cells.
Testicle The part of a boy's body that makes and stores sperm.
Umbilical cord The tube that connects the placenta to the unborn baby.
Uterus The part of a girl where an unborn baby grows.
Vagina The passage that leads from the opening between a girl's legs to her uterus.

General words

Cell The very tiny parts all living things are made of.
Nerves Tiny threads that carry messages to and from your brain.
Organ A group of tissues that work together to do a special job. Your heart is an organ.
System A group of organs that work together. Your heart and blood vessels together make up your blood system.
Tissue A group of cells that look and act the same, such as muscle tissue.

INDEX

This is a fully updated and revised edition.

First published in 1975.
This edition published in 1995 by Usborne Publishing Ltd, Usborne House, 83-85 Saffron Hill, LONDON EC1N 8RT, England.

© Usborne Publishing Ltd 1995, 1992, 1975

Printed in Portugal.